I0845636

Home-Based Wealth

Building Financial Success from Your Living Room

Table of Contents

Chapter 1. Introduction

In our Special Report entitled "Home-Based Wealth: Building Financial Success from Your Living Room", we venture into the exciting world of self-made fortunes, all from the comfort of your home! From successful digital entrepreneurs to brave venturers into stocks and real estate, there's a treasure trove of insights waiting for you, just right inside your living room. We chart the path, step by step, to financial empowerment that isn't based on a 9-to-5 ritual, but on smart, informed decisions you can make right from your cozy couch. Ready to start your wealth-building journey while sipping your favorite cup of coffee? Dive in and discover just how much potential your living room holds to become your personal finance headquarters!

Chapter 2. Understanding Home-based Wealth

The era of the traditional 9-to-5 job is slowly but surely making space for a plethora of home-based ventures that allow individuals to gain wealth in ways more flexible and personalized than ever before. The premise of home-based wealth-building hinges on leveraging your skills, resources, and market opportunities, all while relaxing in your living room.

2.1. Home-Based Wealth: A Broad Overview

Home-based wealth fundamentally refers to the act of generating income or accumulating assets, right from the comfort of your home. It can relate to a range of methods, including running businesses, trading or investing in stocks, buying and leasing real estate, turning hobbies into profitable ventures, blogging, digital freelancing, amongst others.

Working from home has been significantly facilitated by technological innovation. The internet, with its unprecedented connectivity, has turned local businesses into global enterprises, and assets into tradable commodities accessible from your home. Put simply, the world has become your oyster, if you know how to crack it open.

2.2. Identifying Your Niche

Every successful home-based wealth journey starts with identifying your niche. Identifying the right niche is vital as it paves the foundation for your future endeavors. This process involves self-reflection, market research, and strategy planning.

Your abilities, interests, qualifications, and passions hold clues to potential home-based ventures. For instance, if you have always had a knack for painting, turning it into a money-making opportunity may not be as far-fetched as you think. Alternatively, if your professional background lies in finance, you may use that knowledge to trade stocks or consult for businesses.

Market research should go hand-in-hand with self-reflection. Identify opportunities that exist in the marketplace, who your potential customers would be, and how you can best reach out to them. Use online tools like Google Trends, Keyword Planner, and social media analytics platforms.

2.3. Structuring Your Home-Based Business

Once you have identified your niche, the next step involves structuring your business or investment strategy. A solid business structure may include a business plan, marketing plan, and an operations strategy.

A solid business plan outlines your business goals, target market, product or service offerings, pricing strategy, marketing, and sales plan. On the other hand, a solid investment strategy outlines your financial goals, risk tolerance, investment guidelines, and contingency plans.

Next, implement your marketing plan using tools such as social media, website SEO, newsletters, among others. Your operations strategy should detail the daily operations of your at-home business - from sourcing your product or service to delivering it to your customer.

2.4. Leveraging Online Platforms

The success of a home-based venture is heavily dependent on the ability to leverage digital platforms. Be it running an e-commerce store, freelance writing, drop shipping, blogging, or investing in stocks and real estate, digital platforms play a critical role.

Online platforms connect you to potential customers across the globe, provide tools for efficient business management, and enable access to myriad educational resources. Familiarize yourself with platforms relevant to your venture, such as Shopify for e-commerce, Medium for blogging, or Robinhood for stock trading.

2.5. Managing Risks

While home-based wealth generation can yield lucrative returns, it comes with inevitable risks. The risks can be minimized through thoughtful planning, regular monitoring, diversification, and education.

Adopt a risk management plan that identifies potential threats and outlines preventive measures or contingency plans. Regularly monitor your business or investment performance, and make necessary adjustments. Diversify your portfolio or income streams to hedge against potential losses. Finally, continue educating yourself about your niche, market trends, technological advancements, and regulatory changes.

In a nutshell, building home-based wealth requires creativity, strategizing, leveraging available resources, and continually adapting to changes. While it may sound daunting, remember that every venture comes with associated risks. In comparison, home-based ventures offer a note of comfort – you can take control of your financial future while savoring a cup of coffee on your favorite couch!

Chapter 3. Succinct Guide to Financial Management

Managing finances efficiently is the cornerstone of home-based wealth-building. It entails understanding your incoming cash flow, expenditures, investments, debts, and future financial plans efficiently. Amidst the modern world's complexities, Financial Management can feel daunting, but with a systematic approach, you can easily conquer it.

3.1. Understanding Personal Finances

The essential element in effective financial management is to comprehend personal finances. It is necessary to ascertain your income, liabilities, assets, and financial goals.

1. **Income:** It consists of your regular salary, investments, money from part-time jobs, or freelance work. The stability and nature of these streams can vary but combine to form your total income.

2. **Liabilities:** These are financial obligations or debts you owe, such as loans or bills.

3. **Assets:** This includes all your savings, cash, property, investments, etc.

4. **Financial Goals:** These are personal objectives for the future that require financial resources such as buying a home, starting a business, retirement, etc.

An assessment of these factors provides you with a holistic view of your current financial status, laying a foundation for effective management.

3.2. Budgeting and Tracking Spending

After understanding your finances, the next step is to create a budget and track spending. This process involves mapping out your income, controlling your costs, and knowing where you stand.

1. **Income:** Calculate your total earnings for the month.

2. **Fixed Costs:** Identify all costs that don't change from month to month, such as rent, mortgage, and insurance premiums.

3. **Variable Expenses:** Items such as groceries, entertainment, and personal care fall under this category.

4. **Savings and Investments:** Aim to save a portion of your earnings and contribute to a dedicated investment plan.

Regularly evaluating your budget keeps you on track, adjusts your spending habits, and ensures your savings and investments are on target.

3.3. Emergency Fund

The establishment of a safety nest or emergency fund is an integral part of prudent financial management. Setting aside 3-6 months of living expenses can help cushion you from unexpected events like loss of a job, medical emergencies, or sudden significant expenditures. Building and maintaining this fund should take priority over non-essential spending, aiming to achieve a balance between living comfortably today while preparing for the uncertainties of the future.

3.4. Debt Management

Guaranteeing a sound financial status requires thoughtful debt management. Prioritize paying off high-interest rate debt, such as credit cards, to lessen interest payments. Try to maintain low to modest levels of debt relative to your income and avoid unnecessary borrowing. Remember, your overall financial health isn't just about earnings but effectively managing your existing obligations.

3.5. Investment

Investment is the key to growing your wealth. This can include a broad range of opportunities such as stocks, bonds, mutual funds, real estate, etc. Diversification of your investment portfolio can help reduce risk by spreading out your investments over various sectors and instruments. Investment isn't about immediate returns but building long-term growth.

3.6. Retirement Planning

Regardless of your age, retirement planning is a critical component of financial management. The earlier you start, the more time your money has to grow. Consider pension plans, Individual Retirement Accounts (IRA), or employer-sponsored plans like a 401(k).

3.7. Insurance

Protection of your wealth is vital, and insurance plays a crucial role in that. Health, your home, vehicle, and life insurance preserve your assets against unforeseen loss or damage.

3.8. Regular Reviews and Adaptation

Change is the only constant - this applies to your finances as well. Regularly review your financial plan and adapt to changing circumstances like promotion, marriage, children, or retirement.

In conclusion, efficient financial management is a journey, not a destination. By understanding, budgeting, tracking expenses, managing debts, making sound investments, and planning for retirement, you establish the pillars of a solid financial future. Stick to this path and make necessary adjustments over time, you can successfully build financial success from your living room.

Chapter 4. Crafting Your Personal Business Model

The idea of a personal business model isn't new, but its importance has skyrocketed with the advent of the gig economy and home-based businesses.

4.1. Understanding Your Personal Business Model

A personal business model is akin to a roadmap that outlines your goals and objectives, income sources, and strategies to achieve the financial success you desire. It factors in your current skills, passions, resources, and the opportunities available, as much as your risk tolerance.

Understanding the functional specifics of your personal business model requires tremendous introspection. It's where you must look to your strengths and figure out how they can serve as a value proposition, delivering solutions to potential customers.

Once you've identified your value proposition, the next piece of the puzzle is understanding your customer segments. Who are your ideal customers? Why would they be willing to pay for your offerings? What distinguishes you from the competition in their eyes?

Establishing your revenue streams follows this. How will you make money? How much will it cost to produce or provide what you're selling? What kind of profit margin can you expect?

Similarly, take into account any obstacles or key resources that could influence your strategy. This can range from understanding regulations that may affect your operations to identifying the human, financial, and intellectual capital you need and have at your disposal.

4.2. Developing a Customer Value Proposition

This is the segment where you need to be laser-focused on your target audience. An excellent customer value proposition tells your customer why they should buy from you and not your competition. It clearly articulates how you solve your customer's problem, what benefits they can expect, and why they should trust you.

Taking the time to develop this customer value proposition will not only help you identify your target customers but will also highlight ways in which you can innovate and expand your business.

4.3. Finding Your Revenue Streams

Your revenue stream is where your business makes money. There are multiple avenues for home-based businesses, including sales, subscription, leasing, licensing, brokerage fees, and more. The type of revenues you choose depends largely on your business model and the type and size of your customer base.

Identify each source of income, and project possible annual and monthly income. Also, consider what your customers are willing to pay, how they currently pay, how each revenue stream contributes to overall revenues, and whether it's an ongoing or one-time revenue.

4.4. Identifying Key Resources

For your personal business model to be a success, it's necessary to pinpoint the essential resources that will allow your business to create and provide your value proposition, reach your targeted market, maintain a customer relationship, and make a profit.

Key resources can be physical (like your computer) or intangible (like your time and networking capabilities). Also, they can be human (like your skills) or financial (like your seed funding). Don't forget to account for software or applications you'll be needing - these also constitute important resources.

4.5. Acknowledging Potential Challenges

The journey to financial success is not without its hurdles. Acknowledging potential challenges from the start will equip you better to face them.

At the beginning, your most common challenges might be attracting customers, pricing your products/services correctly, managing your time effectively, and battling overwhelm. As your business grows, so too will your challenges. Maintaining quality while scaling, outperforming competitors, navigating legalities, and maintaining cash flow can all become obstacles.

Having a business model that estimates these challenges and is flexible enough to pivot when necessary can help you stay afloat during trying times.

4.6. Model Evolution

No model is set in stone and your personal business model will need to evolve over time as markets, technologies, and customer needs change. Keeping tabs on these shifts will help you update your business model when necessary and stay relevant in a changing landscape.

Keep iterating your business model until you find what works best for you and your customers. Remember, each pivot is a learning opportunity that brings you one step closer to successful and sustainable homeownership.

4.7. Final Words

Constructing a personal business model takes time and careful thought but it comes with enormous rewards. It allows you to proactively direct your financial future, identifying what you want to achieve and how you plan on doing it. It gives you a framework to track your progress, make informed decisions about your future, and understand when and why to make changes. With this, you can turn your living room into a powerhouse for personal financial success.

Chapter 5. Investments and Diversification from Home

By establishing a solid grasp on your finances, you can plant seeds of security for a promising future. And one key way to actualize this vision is by understanding and making the most of the powerful avenue of investments and diversification. Ready to deep dive?

5.1. Beginning with Investments

Investments are essentially purchasing or creating assets with the expectation that value will be gained over time. Investing is not straightforward gambling but is based on assessing risks, monitoring the market, understanding the nuances of different investment avenues, and making informed choices. Various forms of investments range from stocks, bonds, real estate, mutual funds, to even starting your own business venture.

Understanding and undertaking investments might seem complex. However, it becomes relatively simpler once we break it down into why, what, and how of the investing process.

Why Invest?

Money has a tendency to lose its purchasing power over time due to inflation. And simply saving is not enough. Investments can provide you returns that not only outpace inflation but provide wealth generation over time. Therefore, the key reasons to invest include:

- Preserving purchasing power

- Creating wealth

- Achieving financial goals

What to Invest in?

Based on your risk appetite, financial goals, and market dynamics, you could consider the following investment options:

- **Stocks:** If you want to own a piece of a company and share their profitability as well as the risk, investing in stocks is the route you might want to take.

- **Bonds:** These are essentially loaning money to a company or the government. Bonds are less risky compared to stocks as they pay out a fixed interest.

- **Mutual Funds:** These are a basket of different stocks, bonds, or other securities. It allows investors to diversify even with a small amount of money.

- **Real Estate:** Buying property with the anticipation that it will increase in value, either for renting out or for selling at a profit later.

- **Start your own business:** If you have a unique business idea, starting your own venture is another form of investment.

5.2. The How of Investing

Before you make your first investment, you must plan and prepare.

- **Set Clear Financial Goals:** Before setting out, know what you desire to reach. It might be planning for retirement, buying a house, or financing your child's education.

- **Understand your Risk Tolerance:** Every form of investment carries some risk. Your risk tolerance is the degree of uncertainty you are willing to accept in pursuit of your financial objectives.

- **Research is your Best Friend:** Always research your investment targets. What are the prospects of the company? If it's a bond, what's the credit rating?

- **Start Small:** Start by investing a smaller quantity of money, learn, and gradually increase your investment amount.

- **Invest for the Long Term:** The market may be unpredictable in the short-term. But in the long term, it trends upward.

5.3. Power of Diversification

"Diversification" is a buzzword in the investing scene. Investors must diversify their portfolios, which essentially means spreading your investments across different assets classes, to minimize risk.

Why Diversify?

Diversification essentially spreads the risk. By holding different kinds of investments, the negative performance of some investments is cushioned by the favorable performance of others.

Diversification is particularly beneficial in uncertain markets. It ensures losses on certain assets can be offset by gains in others, securing your portfolio against potential losses in any individual investment.

5.4. Building a Diversified Portfolio

The essence of a diversified portfolio is having a mix of assets such as stocks, bonds, and commodities in different sectors and geographic locations. Balanced funds or asset allocation funds can provide a level of diversification.

However, there is no one-size-fits-all approach to building a diversified portfolio. It is unique to each individual and depends on numerous factors such as risk appetite, financial goals, and investment horizon. Consulting a financial advisor or using robo-advising tools can be beneficial in building a balanced portfolio.

Remember, diversification is not 'investing in a lot of things,' it's 'investing in the right combination of things'.

5.5. The Future of Home-Based Investing

As technology progresses, people can now build a fortune from their living rooms. The tools and resources to be a home-based investor are increasingly accessible.

- **Online Brokerage Accounts:** Online brokerages provide you with the platform to manage your portfolio from the comfort of your home.

- **Robo-Advisors:** Robo-advisors use algorithms and machine learning to manage and diversify your portfolio.

- **Investment Apps:** Investment apps have made it even simpler to invest with a swipe of the screen anytime, anywhere.

- **Information Resources:** The internet opens up endless possibilities of information – from market news, analyses, reports to online courses, webinars, and forums.

Investing from home is not only convenient but also empowering. It provides you not only the liberty to invest at your own time and pace but also demands responsibility of staying informed, calculated risk-taking, and continuous learning.

By effectively leveraging technology, you can transform your living room into your personal financial headquarters. Start your investment journey. You don't have to hit the jackpot overnight. Remember, Rome wasn't built in a day. Investing is a marathon, not a sprint. And remember - you're not alone, we are here along with other resources to assist and wake you through. Happy investing from home!

Chapter 6. Online Income Streams: A Deep Dive

The vast digital landscape offers diverse opportunities to generate income from your living room. Whether it's through e-commerce or content creation, a growing number of individuals have tapped into the power of the internet to build sustainable wealth. Let's unravel the intricacies of online income and explore strategies to optimize these revenue streams.

6.1. The Allure of Passive Income

Passive income has been a recurring theme in wealth creation discourses, and there's good reason for this. Passive income refers to earnings derived from sources that require little to no daily effort to maintain. The internet offers a myriad of passive income opportunities, from selling digital products to affiliate marketing.

In the digital world, once the initial work of setting up a passive income source is done, you can earn money on autopilot, even while you sleep. Notice something important, though: the "initial work". Passive income doesn't mean zero effort; it just means that the bulk of the work is front-loaded.

6.2. Selling Digital Products

Creating and selling digital products is one of the most direct and manageable ways to generate online income. We could be talking about eBooks, digital art, printables, music, software, or courses. The beauty of digital products is that they are scalable and can be distributed globally with no additional costs per unit.

1. eBooks: With self-publishing platforms like Amazon Kindle Direct

Publishing, it's never been easier to publish your own eBook and reach a global readership.

2. Digital art and printables: Sites like Etsy and Artstation cater to artists and graphic designers offering a platform to sell their digital creations.

3. Courses: Educational platforms such as Udemy and Coursera offer a marketplace for expert-led courses on a wide array of subjects.

6.3. Affiliate Marketing: The Art of Commission Earning

Affiliate marketing lets you earn a commission by promoting other companies' products. Affiliates usually use their blogs or social media following to recommend products and earn a percentage of sales through affiliate links. Platforms like Amazon Associates, ClickBank, and CJ Affiliate by Conversant provide an extensive range of products to promote.

Affiliate marketing takes time and effort but has great potential. With a niche website or a solid social media following coupled with compelling content, you can earn a steady income.

6.4. Trading Investments: Stocks, ETFs, and Cryptocurrencies

The online world has democratized investing, allowing individuals to buy and sell stocks, ETFs, and cryptocurrencies straight from their homes.

The stock market and especially the world of cryptocurrencies provide lucrative opportunities, but they come with significant risks. Before diving into trading, it's crucial to educate yourself about the market dynamics, and perhaps get some advice from trusted financial experts or use virtual stock trading simulators for practice.

6.5. Building a Personal Brand: Content Creation and Advertising

Building a personal brand through blogs, YouTube, podcasts, or social media platforms can also bring in income through advertising. Google AdSense, YouTube's Partner Program, and sponsored posts on social media platforms are common ways content creators earn money.

The key is to consistently produce high-quality, engaging content that attracts and maintains a following. While it is time-consuming, the potential payoff makes it worthwhile.

6.6. Dropshipping and E-commerce

Dropshipping and e-commerce have surged in popularity in recent years. They involve selling goods online without holding inventory. Through dropshipping, once a sale is made, the product is shipped directly from the manufacturer to the customer.

It requires upfront work like building a website and sourcing products, but once set up, it can quickly become a source of passive income. Shopify and WooCommerce are platforms that offer tools to start a dropshipping business.

6.7. Leveraging the Gig Economy

Freelancing and consulting fall into what is referred to as the "gig economy." Websites like Upwork, Fiverr, and Freelancer connect skilled individuals with businesses seeking their services.

In conclusion, building online income streams involves calculated risks, constant learning and perseverance. The potential to create wealth from the comfort of your living room is huge, but it's crucial to understand that it's not an overnight success. Online wealth generation involves consistent effort, patience, and persistent upskilling.

Chapter 7. Real Estate Investments: Remote Success Stories

When we speak of remote wealth creation strategies in the context of real estate, the conversation inevitably turns towards various levels of property investment, spanning from residential rentals, commercial spaces, to real estate investment trusts (REITs). Each of these strategies has a unique framework and modus operandi, each offering a different level of risk and return.

7.1. A Spotlight on Successful Remote Investors

Linda Roberts, an entrepreneur from Minnesota, started her real estate journey timidly, by renting her two-bedroom townhouse and moving into a smaller apartment.

"Like many, I was drawn to real estate by its tangible nature - it's something you can touch and feel," Linda shares. "In 2012, I rented out my home for the first time and moved into a smaller, cheaper apartment. This strategy, known as house hacking, allowed me to offset my living expenses significantly."

Linda represents a demographic of successful remote real estate investors, leveraging accumulated equity, interest rates, and market trends from the comfort of home. Over eight years, she expanded her portfolio by reinvesting her profits - and today owns ten rental properties across the state.

7.2. Success Tale: Commercial Property's Remote Control

Robert Greene, a digital nomad and tech consultant from Oregon, chose a different approach - commercial real estate. Greene understood that businesses, unlike individuals, are often willing to sign long-term leases, offering more reliable cash flow and decrease vacancy periods.

Starting with a single property - a small, local coffee shop - Greene gradually expanded his portfolio to now include four retail spaces, two office buildings, and a co-working space. Central to his success was the understanding of market trends and intelligent property management, which he handled remotely, leveraging advanced property management software.

"Real estate investing isn't just about owning land," Greene says, "It also involves understanding areas like tax considerations, laws, and keeping up with financial market trends. That's where technology steps in, helping me manage everything from maintenance to payroll."

7.3. Harnessing the Power of REITs: An Retiree's Journey

Marion Phillips, a retiree living in Arizona, found her wealth-building sanctuary in REITs - or Real Estate Investment Trusts, enabling her to invest in real estate without the need to buy or manage a property.

REITs are essentially companies that own, operate, or finance income-generating real estate. They work much like mutual funds, providing a way for individual investors to earn a share of income produced through commercial real estate.

"I wanted a hands-off investment that could supplement my retirement income," Marion explains. "I started investing in REITs about five years ago. They have their risks, like any investment, but by studying the market, I was able to understand which REITs had the potential for profit; the regular dividends were a big bonus."

7.4. A Deep Dive into Tools and Techniques

Whether it's maintaining a rental portfolio, running commercial properties, or investing in REITs, it's essential to keep your finger on the pulse of economics, both local and global. This requires mastering a slew of remote tools and techniques:

1. Property Management Software: Simplifying the rigors of maintaining a property portfolio remotely, these platforms offer features like rent collection, tenant screening, accounting, and more.

2. Public Records: Property records, zoning details, tax data - these records help to make an informed decision.

3. Online Courses: There's never enough knowledge you can imbibe in this field. Look for online courses to recharge your understanding today!

4. Forums & Social Media: Engage with online communities, understand the experiences of others, and learn from their mistakes.

5. Virtual Meetings: They are an excellent tool for talking to potential tenants, contractors, or fellow investors.

7.5. Conclusion

One doesn't have to be present physically to create wealth through real estate. The landscape is evolving, and remote investing is becoming increasingly viable—meditated through technology, enhanced by shared knowledge, and bolstered by regulatory frameworks. Staying informed is key – understanding market trends, legal changes, and technology updates are imperative.

Like Linda, Robert, and Marion, a multitude of people are engineering financial independence using real estate—right from their living room. This thriving phenomenon urges us to consider this alternative avenue to traditional jobs, urging us to break free from our 9-5 rituals.

Remember, real estate is not easy money, but strategic planning, patience, and a keen understanding of the market are likely to yield success. So, here's to your success on your journey to wealth creation, right from the heart of your home - your living room.

Chapter 8. Maximizing Shares and Stocks: The Home Trader's Guide

When it comes to creating wealth from the comfort of your own home, the world of stock trading is, without question, a cornerstone. It's a landscape of immense opportunities, and yet a labyrinth of complexities too. Distilling the insights from successful home traders, this chapter will guide you through the maze, simplifying concepts, and introducing strategies to set you on the path towards becoming a proficient home trader.

8.1. Requisite Knowledge: Understanding Stock Markets

First and foremost, successful trading begins with a solid understanding of the stock market landscape. It's not about captivating jargon and complex equations, but a foundational grasp of the fundamental elements. Understanding the concepts of stock types, indices, economic indicators, and market cycles are essentials on this journey.

Delve into the kinds of stocks: common stocks that give holders voting rights, but make them last in line during company bankruptcy, and preferred stocks that accord no voting rights but prioritize holders during payouts and bankruptcy. Tracing the S&P 500 and Dow Jones Industrial Average gives you a sense of the overall market health. Economic indicators like the GDP give a snapshot of economic progression, while understanding market cycles aids in pinpointing investment timing.

8.2. Instruments: Screen, Validate, Invest

Once your foundation is solid, it's time to grasp the art of choosing your trading instruments. Exploration tools, validation metrics, and investment portfolios are the three weapons to arm yourself with.

Begin by mastering exploratory tools like screeners that filter stocks based on your preferred metrics such as earnings per share (EPS), price-to-earnings (P/E) ratio, and market capitalization. Additionally, understanding technical analysis instruments like Moving Average Convergence Divergence (MACD), Relative Strength Index (RSI), and Fibonacci retracements can help identify potential buy and sell signals.

8.3. Setting Up Your Home Trading Environment

Thinking of plunging into the home-trading sea without a proper ship? Think again. Set up your home trading station with multiple screens or a trading laptop, a stable internet connection, data backup devices, a comfortable chair, and an ergonomic desk. Setting up a successful trading environment goes beyond the physical. It's about discipline — set trading hours, develop consistent habits, continuously learn, and stay updated with news that might affect your stocks.

8.4. Trading Strategies: Choose Your Path

There's no one-size-fits-all trading strategy. Some traders find success with a short-term strategy known as day trading, buying and selling stocks within a single day. Others opt for swing trading, buying and selling over a period spanning several days to weeks. And still, others adopt long-term strategies, holding onto stocks for months or even years in the hope of substantial returns.

Remember, the right strategy isn't just about potential profits. It's about aligning your financial goals, risk appetite, investment capital, and lifestyle preferences. Experiment with different strategies, learn from each trade, and over time, you'll find the right fit.

8.5. Risk Management: Navigating the Churn

Stock trading from home isn't a walk in the park. It's a roller-coaster ride with its euphoric highs and nerve-wracking lows. A well-devised risk management plan helps navigate these extremes. Setting your risk-reward ratio, using stop-losses, and diversifying your portfolio are key ingredients in the recipe for risk management. Don't expect to eliminate all risks, but a good plan reduces them to a level you're comfortable with.

8.6. Emotional Mastery: The Silent Gamechanger

The home trading arena tests not just your financial acumen, but your emotional strength as well. Fear and greed can significantly skew your decision-making abilities. Practicing emotional mastery means being patient when the market moves against you, not rushing into trades, and stepping away when emotions run high.

Embrace the ups-and-downs of stock trading with an open mind, disciplined approach, and an adaptive strategy. With determination, commitment, and continuous learning, you can maximize shares and stocks trading right from your living room. Challenge yourself, control your emotions, and remember that patience is the most rewarding virtue in the world of home trading.

Chapter 9. Home-based Wealth and Your Taxes

Nurturing wealth from the comfort of your living room can come with a multitude of benefits. However, it's critical to note that with newfound financial freedom comes the responsibility of understanding and managing your tax obligations. Each stream of home-based income, be it from online businesses, stock trading, or property investment, has its unique tax considerations. Knowing more about your responsibilities can help avoid any potential legal pitfalls and allow you to effectively manage and grow your wealth.

9.1. Understanding Your Tax Obligations

One of the most important aspects of becoming a home-based wealth-builder is to understand the tax implications of your endeavors. Your tax responsibility will largely depend on the form of your earnings. Remember, your income doesn't simply come under one broad category – the IRS requires that each type be reported differently. Here's a brief overview:

- **Freelance or contract work**: This kind of income is categorized as self-employment earnings and will require you to pay self-employment tax, which covers social security and Medicare.

- **Online selling**: If you're running a home-based eCommerce platform, the tax requirements may differ depending on your revenues and the state you operate from.

- **Investment income**: Income from investments such as stocks, bonds, or mutual funds must be reported as capital gains or losses.

- **Rental income**: Earnings generated from renting out real estate property must also be reported. However, some costs associated with maintaining your rental property, like repairs or mortgage interest, can be deducted from your rental income.

Remember, non-compliance with tax laws can lead to severe penalties, hence the importance of understanding your tax obligations cannot be overstated.

9.2. Navigating Self-Employment Taxes

When pursuing home-based wealth through self-employment, it's important to understand the requirements for self-employment tax. Unlike conventional employment where your employer withholds social security and Medicare taxes, self-employed individuals are responsible for handling these on their own.

Calculating your self-employment tax will depend on your net earnings. The current self-employment tax rate is 15.3%, where 12.4% is for Social Security and 2.9% for Medicare. However, this is subject to caps and additional taxes depending on your annual earnings. You may also be required to make estimated tax payments throughout the year.

Beyond this, self-employed individuals can take advantage of certain deductions, including the home office deduction and deductions for healthcare premiums, which can significantly lower your tax bill.

9.3. Online Selling and Taxes

Operating an online store from your living room? It's crucial to understand how sales taxes apply to your eCommerce activities.

Depending on your state, you may need to collect sales tax from your customers. You're typically required to collect tax for orders delivered within the states where you have "nexus", which includes any location where you operate your business. It can become complex if you sell across states or internationally, so you may want to consider consulting a tax professional to understand your obligations better.

Furthermore, income generated from your eCommerce business is subject to income tax. This income should be reported as business income, and you'll have the opportunity to deduct relevant expenses to lower your tax liability.

9.4. The Tax Impact of Investments

Investments such as stocks, bonds, and mutual funds provide an excellent avenue for home-based wealth generation. However, they also come with their own tax implications.

Any profit you receive when selling an investment is considered a capital gain and is subject to capital gains tax. The rate you pay will depend largely on your income bracket and how long you held the asset before selling. In general, holding investments for at least a year could qualify you for lower long-term capital gains tax rates.

Dividends received from your investments are also taxable. However, "qualified dividends" may be subject to lower tax rates.

Keeping accurate records of your investment activities can make a world of difference during tax season. Document when you bought and sold assets, the price you paid, and any income you received. This will enable you to calculate your capital gains accurately.

9.5. Rental Income and Taxes

Rental income is fully taxable and must be included in your income tax return. However, the IRS allows for several deductions that can offset the rental income you report. These deductions include expenses related to maintaining your rental property, such as repairs, utilities, property taxes, insurance, and mortgage interest.

Keep detailed records of all your rental activities, including income received and expenses occurred. These records will be incredibly useful when it comes to accurately report your rental income and deductible expenses.

9.6. Conclusion

Understanding your tax responsibilities when building wealth from your living room is crucial. It helps not only comply with the law but also allows you to make the most of tax deductions and credits, maintaining more of your hard-earned home-based wealth.

Remember, this guide offers a general overview of some tax obligations tied to home-based income generation. Laws vary widely by location, and individual circumstances can significantly impact your tax situation. For detailed assistance, consider consulting with a tax professional or certified public accountant who can guide you through your specific tax situation and help you effectively plan for your taxes.

Chapter 10. Retirement Planning: Building a Future from Home

Planning for retirement is perhaps the most crucial aspect of financial management that many people neglect until it's too late. With the advent of the digital age and the possibility to build wealth from home, retirement planning can, and should, commence as early as feasible.

10.1. Concept of Building a Retirement Nest Egg

From the word go, understand that having ample money during retirement is not something that happens by chance. Rather, it's a years-long, relentless pursuit that requires sacrosanct discipline, unwavering commitment, informed decision-making, and judicious time management. Think of building your retirement fund as gradually constructing a sprawling mansion, brick by brick. Each decision you make, each money you save, and each compeunded return you receive is another brick on your retirement house. The sooner you start, the more robust and elaborate your retirement mansion will be.

10.2. Sharpen Your Financial Literacy

Your bulletproof weapon in this pursuit is your financial literacy. Grasping the basics of cash-flow management, investing principles, compounding interest, and risk diversification can go a long way in fortifying your retirement strategy. Set apart some time to learn the basics of finance. There are countless online courses and free resources that can help you educate yourself. Prudent decisions made based on sound understanding will help in keeping your retirement journey on track.

10.3. Formulate Your Retirement Plan

Answer these crucial questions: At what age do you wish to retire? What kind of lifestyle do you envisage post-retirement? What would be your monthly expenses? How long do you anticipate to live in retirement? The answers form the foundation of your plan - to compute the total corpus required for retirement. With a clear target, you will better plan your pensions, savings, investments, and insurances.

10.4. Diversify Your Investments

Do not put all your eggs in one basket. Warren Buffet's timeless advice rings true, especially in retirement planning. Diversifying your investments shields you from the capricious volatility of markets. Bonds, stocks, mutual funds, commodities, or real estate - find a balance depending on your risk tolerance.

10.5. Step into Real Estate Investment

Directly buying, flipping, and renting properties may prove daunting for the uninitiated. REITs (Real Estate Investment Trusts) provide a simpler doorway into real estate investment. They distribute dividends and tend to perform relatively stable, making them an enticing option for retirement portfolios. However, nothing replaces the traditional sustainability and tangible appeal of owning a property.

10.6. Buy into the Stock Market

Investments in stocks, over a lengthy period of time, have recorded reasonably high returns. You can consider robo-advisors or a traditional human advisor, depending on your confidence and knowledge of the share markets. A rule of thumb is to subtract your age from 100, and the answer is the percentage that you should invest in stocks.

10.7. Secure Your Future with Bonds

Owning bonds can be an excellent strategy to derive steady cash-flows in retirement. Bonds are essentially less risky than stocks and provide regular payments of fixed interest. Owning bonds of corporations and governments are both possibilities worth exploring.

10.8. Don't Underestimate the Mighty Mutual Fund

Mutual funds are a convenient way of investing in a diversified portfolio curated by investment professionals. Choosing funds that have consistently beaten market averages can supply attractive compounding over the years. Passive index funds are also a great low-cost alternative.

10.9. Stick to Your Plan and Regularly Review It

Design your plan such that it motivates you to save and invest relentlessly month after month. Your plan must chart a clear path to reach your target corpus. At the same time, periodically reviewing your strategy allows you to re-adjust the path to compensate for unexpected changes or to optimize better opportunities in markets or tax laws.

Retirement planning isn't a walk in the park. But with the right attitude, ample discipline, and smart decisions, you can build a future that doesn't require giving up on life's tiny pleasures. As you reap the benefits of your labor, you'll come to realize that your home sweet home was indeed the perfect place to hatch this splendid pursuit.

To turn your retirement journey into a quest teeming with excitement and profound fulfillment, remember this: Start early, stay invested, and remember, Rome – like a robust retirement plan – wasn't built in a day!

Chapter 11. Keeping the Balance: Home Wealth and Personal Life

The beauty of building wealth at home is developing the perfect blend of personal and professional life. This delicate equilibrium requires apt management and planning. The equilibrium is often offset by personal distractions or professional demands. However, with a few essential pivots in your journey, you can master this balance and live a well-rounded, fulfilling life while accumulating wealth from the comfort of your living room.

11.1. Gearing Up For Home-Based Wealth Creation

Starting out on home-based wealth generation involves discerning financial planning and goal setting. Plan your operations meticulously, allocating time and resources adeptly within your home. Pen down your financial goals and assign timelines, breaking them down into achievable actions.

For instance, if your path involves investing in stocks, determine your financial targets, decide on risk parameters and establish the time you will dedicate for research and analysis. Comply with these parameters religiously. Remember to make room for personal time in your schedule.

11.2. Setting Boundaries

Research illustrates that entrepreneurs who set distinct boundaries between their work and personal life are more successful. Set your workspace apart in your home, away from distractions. When you're in this space, commit to your work. But once you step out, let your focus gravitate back towards your personal life. This clear demarcation can help dissolute the blurred lines between work and leisure, ensuring that familial relationships remain untaxed.

11.3. Balancing Financial Risk and Rewards

Financial risk and rewards reside on two ends of a spectrum. Striking a balance between them involves leveraging your financial literacy, patience, and readiness to embrace risks. Define your risk tolerance, considering your financial situation and investment goals. It's also crucial to diversify your investment portfolio - spreading your wealth across different asset classes offers a safety net against potential market downturns.

11.4. Handling Emotional Stress

Managing your wealth from home incorporates an understated emotional aspect. This realm involves egos, insecurities, and anxieties, which often interfere with logical decision-making. Consider outsourcing financial coaching or psychological counseling to maintain your emotional health. Self-care activities such as exercise, hobbies, and social engagements can also aid in managing stress and staying motivated.

11.5. Time Management

Learning to manage time effectively is a vital skill to maintain the balance between work and personal life. Allocate specific hours for your wealth-building activities, personal commitments and leisurely pursuits. By outputting stringent time slots for various tasks, it is possible to heighten productivity and ward off procrastination.

11.6. Regular Involvement vs. Passive Income

Regular involvement in your home-based wealth creation activities is pivotal, but generating passive revenue streams will ensure consistent cash flow. Investments in real estate, dividend stocks, or P2P lending platforms can provide a steady income source without demanding your regular attention, allowing you to focus on other aspects of your life.

11.7. Embracing Flexibility

Rigidness can lead to burnout. Embrace a flexible lifestyle which allows fluctuations in your work schedule. If you have a pressing personal commitment, it's acceptable to adjust your work obligations accordingly.

11.8. Maintaining Personal Relationships

Isolation is a common pitfall of home-based entrepreneurs. Maintain your personal relationships and ensure that you allocate time for friends and family. After all, wealth creation doesn't equate to happiness if relationships get strained.

Home-based wealth generation is a promising approach to gaining financial independence. It enables you to enjoy the freedom and flexibility that traditional jobs often lack. However, like all good things, it requires effort, discipline, and commitment. Remember, maintaining balance is the key to prevailing in this endeavor, making your living room a powerhouse of productivity and prosperity.

www.ingramcontent.com/pod-product-compliance
Lightning Source LLC
Chambersburg PA
CBHW071044260726
48661CB00007B/3157